CW01209455

ONE MOMENT IN TIME

happy yak

To Elijah and Idris - B.L.
To Chan and Natan - A.S.

Quarto is the authority on a wide range of topics.
Quarto educates, entertains and enriches the lives of our readers—enthusiasts and lovers of hands-on living.
www.quartoknows.com

© 2021 Quarto Publishing plc
Text © Ben Lerwill
Illustrations © Alette Straathof

Ben Lerwill has asserted his right to be identified as the author of this work.
Alette Straathof has asserted her right to be identified as the illustrator of this work.

First published in 2021 by Happy Yak,
an imprint of The Quarto Group.
The Old Brewery, 6 Blundell Street,
London N7 9BH, United Kingdom.
T (0)20 7700 6700 F (0)20 7700 8066
www.quartoknows.com

No part of this publication may be reproduced, stored in a retrieval system, or transmitted in any form, or by any means, electrical, mechanical, photocopying, recording or otherwise, without the prior written permission of the publisher or a licence permitting restricted copying. In the United Kingdom such licences are issued by the Copyright Licensing Agency, 5th Floor, Shackleton House, 4 Battle Bridge Lane, London SE1 2HX.
All rights reserved.

A catalogue record for this book is available from the British Library.

ISBN: 978 0 7112 6351 2

Manufactured in Singapore COS062021
9 8 7 6 5 4 3 2 1

Ben Lerwill · Alette Straathof

ONE MOMENT IN TIME

happy yak

Did you know that day and night happen at different times in different parts of the world?

When it's breakfast time for you, it's bedtime for children on the other side of the world. And when they have their breakfast, you're fast asleep!

Every part of the world has morning, afternoon and evening at different times.

Let's travel around the world and take a look...

It's 7 o'clock in the morning in Mexico. Javier is eating his breakfast. He's having corn tortillas with beans, and a glass of orange juice.

Look at the food and drink in Javier's kitchen. Which of these things do you have in your home?

And at exactly the same time...

... it's 8 o'clock in the morning in New York City.
Kayla is getting her schoolbag ready.

A yellow school bus will take her to the school gates.

Some children around the world have to make very unusual journeys to school - crossing rivers in boats, riding on horseback or even climbing mountains. What are the different ways that people get to your school?

And at exactly the same time...

... it's 9 o'clock in the morning in Brazil. Lucas is having a maths lesson. The time zones might change as you travel around the world, but the times tables don't!

1 × 4 =
2 × 4 =
3 × 4 =
4 × 4 =
5 × 4 =

um dois três

In Brazil, children speak Portuguese. Instead of "one, two, three", they say "um, dois, três". Do you know any numbers from other languages?

And at exactly the same time...

... it's 12 noon in Ghana. Esther is lining up in the schoolyard for her lunch. Today she's having rice, fish and greens.

Esther goes to a school that has a uniform, but at some schools around the world children wear their everyday clothes. Does your school have a uniform? And if you could design your own school uniform, what would it look like?

And at exactly the same time...

... it's 1 o'clock in the afternoon in Scotland.
James is having a music lesson.
He's learning how to play the guitar.

James enjoys playing his guitar. He practises before and after every lesson, because he knows it's the best way to improve. What are the things that you like practising?

And at exactly the same time...

… it's 2 o'clock in the afternoon in Italy.
Francesca is playing football with her class.

She's just scored a goal! Francesca and her friends love playing football because it's fun and it keeps them fit. What are your favourite sports?

And at exactly the same time...

... it's 3 o'clock in the afternoon in Turkey.
Yusuf is borrowing a book from the library.

The book is full of stories and facts. At home, Yusuf likes curling up on his bed to read. Do you have a special place where you like reading?

And at exactly the same time...

... it's 4 o'clock in the afternoon in Dubai. Habiba is making a model of a spaceship.

There are children in every country, and lots of them like the same things. If you were playing with a child from another part of the world, what would you like to do together?

And at exactly the same time...

... it's 5 o'clock in the afternoon in India.
Meera is flying a kite in the hills.

Here in India, the days are often hot and sunny – but sometimes they get very rainy! What's the weather like where you live? Do you have a mix of sun and rain too?

And at exactly the same time...

... it's 7 o'clock in the evening in Thailand.
Arthit is brushing his teeth.

Arthit knows how important it is to keep his teeth clean. Just like you, he brushes them every morning and evening. What else do you do when you're getting ready for bed?

And at exactly the same time...

... it's 10 o'clock at night in Australia.
Suzy is fast asleep.

Millions of children around the world are sleeping right now, while you're reading this book. Does Suzy have things in her bedroom that you have in yours?

And at exactly the same time...

... back in Mexico, Javier is still having his breakfast!

Eleven different children.

One moment in time.

One world, one moment

Our moment in time has taken us right around the world, from Mexico all the way to Australia. On this map we can see the different children that we've met. Can you find where *you* live?

New York City

Mexico

Brazil

Day and night

There's one big reason why different places have day and night at different times – because the world's always turning! This means that when half the world is facing the sun, the other half is facing away from it. When your part of the world turns to face the sun, it's daytime.

How fast does the world turn?

The world is spinning very slowly. It takes 24 hours – or one whole day – for our planet to turn all the way round.

Scotland

Turkey

Italy

Dubai

India

Thailand

Ghana

Australia

A note from the author

Have you ever watched the sun go down in the evening? Or seen it peep above the hills in the morning? It looks like the sun's travelling across the sky – but actually, we're the ones that are moving!

Our amazing planet is always turning, bringing day and night to different parts of the world. Even now, while you're reading this book, children around the world are doing all sorts of different things. Some are asleep. Some are climbing trees. Some are looking up at the stars, others are playing in the sunshine. And the sun that warms their skin is the same sun that warms yours.

No matter where we live, time ticks by at the same speed for all of us. Sixty seconds in a minute. Sixty minutes in an hour. Twenty-four hours in a day. And a day lasts exactly as long in a busy city in America as it does on the wide open plains of Australia.

So the next time you watch the hands ticking around a clock, maybe try and imagine what children in other places are doing. We might not all have our mornings and evenings at the same time – but we all share the same sun, and live under the same sky.

Ben

Alette